FAIRY HOUSES

ALL YEAR

FAIRY HOUSES
❧ ALL YEAR ❧

{ *A Four-Season Handbook* }

LIZA GARDNER WALSH
Photographs by Amy Wilton

Down East Books

Published by Down East Books
An imprint of Globe Pequot
Trade division of The Rowman & Littlefield Publishing Group, Inc.
4501 Forbes Boulevard, Suite 200, Lanham, Maryland 20706
www.rowman.com

Unit A, Whitacre Mews, 26-34 Stannary Street, London SE11 4AB, United Kingdom

Distributed by NATIONAL BOOK NETWORK

Design by Lynda Chilton, Chilton Creative

British Library Cataloguing in Publication Information Available

Library of Congress Cataloging-in-Publication Data Available

ISBN 978-1-60893-580-2 (cloth : alk. paper)
ISBN 978-1-60893-581-9 (electronic)

∞™ The paper used in this publication meets the minimum requirements of American National Standard for Information Sciences—Permanence of Paper for Printed Library Materials, ANSI/NISO Z39.48-1992.

Printed in the United States of America

To my dear friend Sandy,
my fairy godmother. Forever
in my heart.

{TABLE *of* CONTENTS}

Introduction, *The Seasons of Fairy House Building*.............9

Seasonal Disclaimer, *12*

Rules of Fairy House Building, *14*

How to Build a Fairy House in One Easy Lesson, *18*

Things to Collect All Year, *23*

SPRING **24**

Spring Has Sprung and the Fairies Are Busy, *27*

Fairies in Spring, *28*

What to Collect in Spring, *36*

Spring Fairy House Projects and Furnishings, *40*

Spring Fairy Houses, *47*

SUMMER **50**

    Ah, Sweet Summer, *53*

    Fairies in Summer, *54*

    What to Collect in Summer, *58*

    Summer Fairy House Activities, Projects, and Furnishings, *60*

    Summer Fairy Houses, *68*

FALL **74**

    Quiet as a Gently Falling Leaf, *77*

    Fairies in Fall, *78*

    What to Collect in Fall, *84*

    Fall Fairy House Projects and Furnishings, *86*

    Fall Fairy Houses, *91*

WINTER **94**

    The Nip and Chill of the Air, *97*

    Fairies in Winter, *98*

    What to Collect in Winter, *102*

    Winter Fairy House Projects and Furnishings, *105*

    Winter Fairy Houses, *114*

Conclusion, *Fairy Houses Every Day* **117**

Resources **119**

Introduction
The Seasons of Fairy House Building

M ost often when we picture fairies, we imagine them bathed in dappled summer light, clothed in sheer cobweb shawls and flower petal dresses—not hats and scarves and snow suits. But what if they do wear warm clothes and play in snow or leaf piles just as often as they take care of the flowers? There is certainly a chance at any time of year that the fairies are outside—in the rain, shivering in the early morning frost, or hiding from the strong summer sun. If they are outside every day in any weather, you can help them by making a fairy house any day of the year.

Perhaps you've already built a fairy house or maybe even an entire fairy village. Maybe you've always wanted to build one but the weather never seemed quite right. Most often when we build these little houses, we do it in fair weather, often in summer. It is true that fairies love summer, let's face it,

who doesn't? But there is no reason this magical activity needs to be limited only to summer. Every day can be a fairy-house-building day whether there is snow on the ground or a light rain falling. One of the best things about building a fairy house is that it pulls you outside and allows you to think about something other than whether your sister was sharing her favorite Legos or if you got a smaller brownie. When you are in the world of fairy houses there are endless possibilities. Sticks become magic street lights topped with the flowers known as Chinese lanterns, bark becomes a gateway to a fairy pet store, and a snow covered rock or stump can be a fairy sledding hill.

This book not only celebrates the differences of each season but provides lists of things to gather, projects specific to the time of year, things to do, and ways to take care of the fairies all year long. Also included are quotes from fairy experts like you, because, as you probably already guessed, kids know more about fairies than anyone. And there are even stories about certain fairies that like the crunching sound of footsteps through leaf piles and winter fairies that can always find a lost traveler.

As you read and build, remember that one of the most important things for you to do in this fairy house work is to believe in fairies. Another thing is to follow this basic rule of fairy work: if you take care of the world around you and are gentle with nature, the fairies will trust you. There is nothing fairies like more than watching kids delight in the treasures of nature. And you better believe they are watching you! Because as you finish each masterful fairy house, they most likely are climbing through the tiny door and taking a little nap, happy as can be! As you build them a house, no matter whether it is cold, hot, or rainy, they might flutter by. You will know their presence because the hairs on the back of your neck will rise or you might develop a slight case of the goosebumps. You might even hear bells or faint wind chimes, the grass might bend, or you might even see tiny footprints in the snow. But despite the potential sighting of a fairy, despite the importance of making our world better by keeping joy and creativity in your heart, you must understand that this is work that needs to be done often and in all types of weather and places.

Seasonal Disclaimer

Not everyone lives in places where deep snowdrifts hang around until March or where fiery colored leaves drop from the trees beginning in early October. Some of you live in kind climates that may only get a touch windier and a tad cooler in winter. Some places that are close to the equator have very sneaky seasons that only the people who live there notice, for example a little more rain in May. But even if this is the case for you, paying attention to the changes around you and the shifts in nature is one of the best side effects of a life spent building these tiny houses. As you fine tune your observations, you will notice that new building materials continually emerge as the days pile on each other. Milkweed pods empty themselves, flowers bloom, and different types of grasses grow. So although this book roots itself in the traditional four seasons of northern climates, it really is meant for anyone, anywhere, with a good imagination and the ability to notice the natural changes in the world around them.

Rules of Fairy House Building

I know that something so free and fun shouldn't have a bunch of pesky rules, but there are just a few things to keep in mind so that as you build, you also show your respect for nature. The most important rule of all, the one that fairies take very seriously, is not to bring man-made materials into your fairy house. This is a hard one because the fairies do love glittery and shiny things, but not in the realm of nature. What happens is that when lots of man-made things end up in the forests, beaches, or parks, animals and birds might mistake them for food or they end up as litter. Natural materials break down over time, but man-made items like marbles, do not. So that is the biggest rule; here are a few others to help keep nature safe:

- ⚇ Do not pull up moss from the ground. Moss takes many years to grow. For example, pincushion moss can take up to forty years to regenerate if it is disturbed.

- ⚇ Never pull bark from a tree. Bark is basically a tree's skin and if you rip that off, the tree will be vulnerable to disease and weather.

- ⚇ Do not pick flowers from a garden that is not yours unless you have permission. Fairies absolutely adore flowers and, with permission, they are a great living thing that is okay to pick for your fairy house.

CREATE AN ALL-YEAR FAIRY-HOUSE JOURNAL

Buy or make a book with blank pages to be your All-Year journal. As each season passes make lists of the materials you find in your yard or on family walks to the park. Note the differences that you see each season and how your fairy houses change throughout the year. Then draw every fairy house after you build them. Or take photos, print them out, and glue or tape them into your book. Maybe the fairies will write you letters and you can keep them in this journal. And don't forget to write down the signs that fairies have visited.

❦ If you are in a national or state park or state beach it is against the law to remove any natural thing.

❦ Be careful of poison ivy, especially in the summer when it is much harder to see than when it turns red in the fall. Remember the poem, "leaves of three, let it be."

❦ And one more thing, if you are in nature, certain bugs might find you inviting. Always check yourself for ticks after your time in the woods. No one likes ticks, not even fairies.

How to Build a Fairy House in One Easy Lesson

STEP 1: Find a good spot. Fairies need plenty of privacy and protection from wind, dogs, and big feet. Lots of kids are drawn immediately to a certain tree hollow or a space in a stone wall. The beauty of a fairy house site is that, unlike for a human house, the ground does not need to be level. In fact, your house does not even need to be on the ground. Some good examples of fairy

house sites are: tree hollows, tree roots and uprooted trees, stone walls, beaches, stumps, and flower gardens.

STEP 2: Gather your supplies. Throughout the book, there are various lists of things to collect as well as what to use to collect your supplies in. But most importantly, to start make sure you have a good pile of bark to form your walls.

STEP 3: Start to build. Here are a couple of the most common techniques for starting your fairy house construction. You can lean bark or sticks up against a tree, rock, or stone wall creating a lean-to type fairy house. You can balance bark in an A-frame shape where the tops of the bark connect. Or you might find

a perfect hollow in a tree and not need to build walls at all.

STEP 4: Think about the furniture next. Fairies need a bed to take naps in, but what else do you want in there? Do they need a toilet?

STEP 5: Now step back and look at your creation and the entrance to your house. Can you make a grand pathway of tiny pinecones to steer fairies your way? Or a sea glass and sea shell patio? Do you have a fairy door? Last of all, make sure the area around your house is tidy. Fairies are extraordinarily neat creatures and when they see that you have cleaned up all the extra debris in the messy woods, their hearts will sing with joy!

STEP 6: Continue to watch your house and fix it up after it rains and the wind blows. Check for signs that fairies have visited.

STEP 7: Repeat often any day of the year!

Things to Collect All Year

If you are serious about this hobby, then having a constant eye for collecting is a must. Fairy house materials abound in every season. I suggest getting a sturdy bag or box to use when gathering your supplies. I have created a specific fairy house kit that has a handle and four compartments—it is like a briefcase for your fairy house work. (Find them at *mossandgrove.com*.) You can also designate a certain drawer or a shoe box to keep your treasures in so that every surface of the house isn't covered with sticks, shells, rocks, and dried leaves.

In each section, I have listed things to gather that are particularly abundant in that season, for example, dried milkweed pods in winter. But there are many items that you can gather any time of year, such as shells, pine cones, bark (remember to never pull from a tree), feathers, sticks, dried flowers, wool, rocks, mica, sea glass, and grasses. Another great item for fairy houses is a wood round, also known as a tree

slice. You will need a grown up who has access to a saw to help you make these. Whatever you do, remember to stick with natural materials and never use any iron in your fairy house–fairies will not go near a fairy house that has iron in it.

SPRING

"There are fairies at the bottom
of our garden! It's not so very,
very far away."
—ROSE FYLEMAN

THE FAIRY DEW DROP

Down by the spring one morning
Where the shadows still lay deep,
I found in the heart of a flower
A tiny fairy asleep.

Her flower couch was perfumed.
Leaf curtains drawn with care,
And there she sweetly slumbered,
With a jewel in her hair.

But a sunbeam entered softly
And touched her as she lay
Whispering that twas morning
And fairies must away.

All colors of the rainbow
Were in her robe so bright
As she danced away with the sunbeam
And vanished from my sight.

"Twas while I watched them dancing,
The sunshine told me true
That my sparkling little fairy
Was lovely Drop O' Dew.
—LAURA INGALLS WILDER

Spring

Has Sprung and the Fairies Are Busy.

One of the best moments of the year is seeing that first crocus pop up through the recently thawed ground—a shot of color that lets us know spring is officially here. Seeing those first flowers is like a celebratory parade, complete with trumpets and drums. It is truly enchanting to suddenly see green sprouts where before only brown and gray colored our world. Slowly the light returns and days stretch so that you can play outside longer after you get home from school. Everything begins to feel busy in spring after the slowness of winter's rest. Day by day the earth softens and out of it new life emerges. Worms peek out. Peepers make their peeping sounds. Tiny fiddleheads coil outward. Eggshells crack. Baby birds chirp. Green fresh leaves unfurl.

Everywhere people begin the giant task of clearing away winter's debris

—the fallen limbs from heavy snowfalls and last year's dead and dried-out flowers and grasses. Gardens become waiting places as tiny buds slowly poke out their heads. What better time to make a fairy house! For just as the flowers are waking up after winter, so are the fairies. And they are busy! So let's get started—grab a May basket or a bucket, put on some rain boots, and let the building begin.

Fairies in Spring

Imagine you are just a tiny fairy and grass is bursting up all around you—a heavy coat of pollen fills the air, giving it a powdery glow and the world a misty, magical feel. Spring is one of the fairies' favorite seasons, second only to summer. All that new life really gets to the heart of the essential fairy nature. In fact, the entire month of May is known as fairy month. The first of May, also known as May Day, is when the fairies bring presents to the fairy queen and a giant celebration follows. But even before May, the best possibility that you will see

THINGS TO NOTICE IN SPRING

- grass gradually turning green
- the order that the flowers appear
- forsythia, lilacs, peonies, poppies, daffodils, tulips, crocuses, ferns
- pussy willows, cattails
- baby birds and bird nests
- animal tracks in the mud
- caterpillars, tadpoles
- apple tree blossoms
- sound of peepers
- longer days

a fairy will be in the spring. The main reason is that the Spring Equinox, when the seasons officially change on March 21, is considered by fairies to be a "tween time." They love these times when things aren't completely one way or the other. In spring, the natural world is not fully asleep, as in winter, nor fully awake, as in summer. Plus, fairy babies are often born in spring. They sit in the heart of new flowers like little pearls or tiny glass bubbles. According to author Michelle Rohm McCann, author of *Finding Fairies,* if you see flowers bobbing in your garden they might be bowing to an "unseen fairy princess." A sudden gust of wind "might be the royal fairy parade passing by."

The early part of the season, when the air is still cool and the

TIP

Spring can be very windy, so don't be surprised or discouraged if the wind takes your fairy house and scatters it throughout your back yard.

ground hasn't quite filled with new plants, is a good time to look for fairy mounds. A fairy mound is a small rise in the ground, and if you place your ear to one of these mounds, you just might hear the fairies' ethereal music playing.

As I mentioned earlier, the fairies are busy in spring protecting the fragile new plants, raising baby fairies, and helping the animals emerge from hibernation. Flower fairies are assigned to take care of their new flowers, birds ask the fairies for help

as they make their nests, and butterflies give flight tips to baby fairies.
You can be a part of this spring busi-
ness by giving the fairies and nature a
little present—the present of a fairy
house! According to Cicely Mary
Barker, each fairy represents a different flower. They dress in the petals
or leaves of that particular plant or
flower and give their spirit completely to its care. They even take

on the personality of that flower and protect it with all their might. Here is what Cicely Mary Barker has to say about these special flower fairies:

A flower fairy's job is to look after her plant, tending leaves and trimming flowers. A flower fairy is 2-4 inches tall, and has a pair of delicate wings. She, although a flower fairy can be a boy too, dresses in the leaves and flowers from her plant to help her stay hidden. A flower fairy is not at all fussy about where she lives: hanging baskets, window-boxes, a tiny crack in a crumbling wall, or between the pavement stones where weeds and mosses grow—any of these places might be home to a flower fairy. Since almost every-one has a potted plant, or can see a patch of grass, or treetops from their window, this means that almost everyone is close to a flower fairy even if they don't realize it at the time.

Did you hear that, everyone is close to a flower fairy. Especially in spring!

What to Collect in Spring

The great thing about finding fairy house supplies in spring is that as the snow recedes all kinds of treasures emerge. You might even find a mitten or two, your missing lunch box, and even that bouncy ball that bounced away right as you got home from a birthday party. But you will also find tons of natural materials leftover from summer and fall that were hidden by winter. Spring is also a good time to collect sticks to have on hand for a full year of fairy house building, as winter storms pull many branches down. Here is a list of some of the things that are abundant in the spring and are great to add to your fairy house supply chest:

- leftover dried grasses, flowers, dried-out milkweed pods, reeds

- pussy willows, dandelions

- fallen petals, especially poppy petals and poppy pods when the flowers have finished blooming

- egg shells, feathers, rocks

- bark—again, winter is hard on trees, so often there are big chunks of bark in the woods. Remember to never pull bark from a living tree

- abandoned birds' nests

SOME EXTRA THINGS TO DO FOR FAIRIES IN SPRING

- plant flowers to attract butterflies
- laugh and frolic in nature
- be tender with new gardens and do not walk through them
- grow bluebells, fairies favorite flowers
- make mud pies and get dirty
- fix up any fairy houses that have been damaged by the winter

Candied Violets

Excerpted from *Taste of Home*

One of the earliest spring flowers is the violet. Fairies have a special relationship to this flower as it is a favorite of the fairy queen and used in almost all of the spring celebrations. This recipe works only if you use the wild purple violets and not the houseplant called African violet.

TIME: Preparation takes about 20 minutes and baking time is 30 minutes.

INGREDIENTS: 2 egg whites, at least 1 cup of sugar, 1 large bunch of washed wild violets (including stems)

DIRECTIONS:
1. In a bowl, beat egg whites with a wire whisk until they become frothy.
2. Pour sugar into another bowl.
3. Pick up one violet by the stem, then dip into egg whites, making sure to cover all surfaces.
4. Gently dip the violet into the sugar, making sure all of the petals are completely covered.
5. Place on waxed paper-lined baking sheets; then snip off stems.
6. Using a toothpick, open petals to original shape.
7. Sprinkle sugar on any uncoated areas.
8. Dry in a 200-degree oven for 30–40 minutes or until sugar crystalizes.
9. Gently remove violets to wire racks with a spatula or two-tined fork.
10. Sprinkle again with sugar if violets appear syrupy.
11. Cool. Store in airtight containers with waxed paper between layers.

Spring Fairy House Projects and Furnishings

FAIRY BED

You can make a fairy bed in a number of ways. It is one of the most essential and fun accessories in a fairy house. This is just one example because there are no limits to how to make a fairy bed.

- Find a piece of birch bark that is relatively flat.

- Using scissors, cut a semi-circle out of the bark.

- Gather berries, small shells, bright flowers, or sea glass, and arrange a design on the piece of bark.

- Heat your glue gun—remember to have an adult with you while using one.

- Use your glue gun to attach your design onto the bark. This is the head board for your bed.

- Now, find a stick that is about as thick as your thumb and break it into three pieces, two long pieces and one the same width as the head board.

- Use your glue gun to build a frame. Place the two longer pieces on each side of the head board and the shorter branch on the top and bottom.

🌀 Fill the frame with moss, lambs ear, leaves, or flower petals and your fairies will have a wonderful rest!

In spring, it is particularly wonderful to fill your bed with the fragrant petals from a lilac bush. The purple and white flowers will entice any fairy to stop what they are doing and come for a snooze!

DANDELION CHAINS

The great thing about making dandelion chains is that in the spring no one ever minds if you pick a dandelion from their yards because boy, are they plentiful! Another great perk to wearing a dandelion chain is that it will keep away mischievous fairies, allowing you to look festive without being bothered by fairy trouble.

Scour the yard for dandelions with very thick and long stems. Using your fingernail, slice a one-inch tear through the stem. Thread another dandelion through this hole. Then take your fingernail and slice through this next dandelion and thread a new dandelion through. Continue until your chain is the length for a crown or a necklace. Or you can go for the dandelion chain world record like my daughters do each year.

FAIRY CLOTHESLINE

In spring, the fairies are busy washing everything from winter and making new clothes for the summer parties to come. They love to do laundry and with the fresh spring air, they are anxious to hang out their laundry again. Most craft stores carry tiny clothespins for this purpose. To make a clothesline, find two sticks that are about four inches tall and string a piece of yarn across them. Clip your tiny clothespins on the line and maybe hang some rose petals to inspire the fairies to get to work!

WELCOME SIGN

Just in case the fairies spent the winter in Florida, they might need help finding their old fairy houses. It is always a nice idea to welcome them with some kind of a sign. Popsicle sticks cut in half work well for writing messages on and you can even glue on some tiny sea shells to jazz things up. Glue your sign onto a stick and plant it right in front of your fairy house so the fairies will know right where to go!

FAIRY DOOR

The winds of March and the rains of April make a fairy door essential for spring fairy houses. A door is simple to make out of bark with a tiny acorn cap or a berry glued on for a knob. Or you can glue a bunch of sticks that are all the same size together into a larger rectangle and then attach a sea-shell knob. Birch bark

A group of children at Peopleplace Cooperative Preschool had this to say about spring fairies:

They sleep in the day and are out at night.

They like daffodils, moon flowers, and red flowers.

One time Elsie saw a fairy smelling a yellow fairy.

can be cut into a rectangular shape or an arched shape. You can even cut out little windows so the fairies can see who is knocking.

Spring Fairy Houses

DANDELION DEN

This fairy house is an altar to early spring. The fairies will delight in the dandelions enveloping this structure. They will sit at the table underneath a garland of dandelions gazing at the changing spring light and think about all of the festivals to come.

FORSYTHIA FORT

One of the first signs of spring in northern climates is blooming forsythia bushes. These vibrant yellow shrubs make perfect arches for spring fairy houses. One of the best features of a large patch of forsythia is that it provides a hideaway spot for children, small animals, and fairies. So

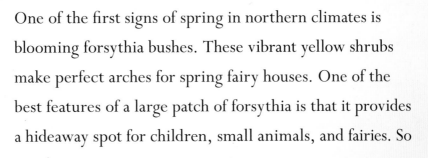

what better site for a fairy house than to be tucked beneath these golden spears? Ask a parent if it is okay to snip a few branches for your fairy house. Use the bright yellow flowers to line pathways, decorate doorways, and fill fairy beds. You can even weave forsythia branches to make the fairy house extra sturdy.

LILAC LAIR

Fairies adore the fragrance of flowers. Once they step into a fairy house coated in the spring scent of lilacs they will be immediately captivated and most likely not want to leave!

Again, you will need to ask permission to cut a few stalks of a lilac bush before you begin this type of fairy house. The branches of the lilac are packed with tiny blossoms and can often be quite large. Placing a few branches next to each other will create a very private hideout for the fairies. Also, placing the varying purple and white flowers in a pile makes a perfect fairy bed. Imagine how heavenly resting on a bed of perfume flowers would be.

SUMMER

AUGUST

August—the time of ripeness,
the corn glowing,
the berries all ripening.

The magpie stands guard,
watching the bilberries,
the raspberries,
blackberries,
cranberries,
and gooseberries,
the red and black currants,
the whortleberries,
cloudberries and more.

They dance in a ring,
the berry Queen smiling,
clad in her August array.
And the magpie
he just watches,
hungrily.
—ELSA BESKOW

Summer

Ah, sweet summer.

This is truly the time that fairies and children wait for all year long. Parties, visits from the fairy queen, and the much anticipated Summer Solstice. We all dream of the endless warm days of summer, and when they arrive, summer often takes on a frenzied fever. The flowers bloom like crazy. Colors are everywhere. You can swim. Oh yeah, and there is no school, which means long days at the beach or pool sipping lemonade. There is so much to enjoy about summer—family picnics, fireworks, boats, time spent in parks. One of the best parts of summer is the music of nature; the bird orchestra that strums to life in the early dawn and the cricket chorus that closes out the day. Windows are open so the happy shouts of your neighbors can be heard, enticing you to go outside and play. Life is at its busiest and most active for all of us, including the fairies.

Fairies in Summer

Fairies love nothing more than adding their special fairy magic to the parties and festivals of summer. They celebrate the long days, eat delicious fairy food, sing gentle songs underneath the glow of the moon and soft light of fireflies, and wear dresses woven from dew and spider-webs. Then, in the warm summer mornings, tucked cozily in their flower-scented beds, they sleep the day away awaiting the next cele-bration. Fairies like summer best, and I bet that when they watch kids building them fairy houses, it makes them like it even more! Making a fairy world can be elaborate in summer because with the warm weather you get to stay outside even

THINGS TO NOTICE IN SUMMER

- tidal changes
- shells and sea glass
- roses, Queen Anne's lace
- monarch butterflies
- giant hosta leaves
- honeysuckle
- bees, ants, beetles, and mosquitoes
- hummingbirds
- dragonflies
- the bird orchestra
- thunderstorms
- crickets and cicadas
- snails and snail trails

longer. You can do amazing things when the weather is on your side, like some kids I know named Field, Adele, and Violet Griffith, who made things like a fairy cemetery, a pet store, a fairy desert island with treasure, a fairy jewelry store, and even a fairy slide park! There are so many materials to use in summer for fairy house building, but this is truly when nature's bounty is

SOME EXTRA THINGS TO DO FOR THE FAIRIES IN SUMMER

🐝 attend a fairy festival

🐝 tell your friends about making fairy houses and do it together

🐝 visit a botanical garden or a fairy trail in your community and add your own fairy houses

🐝 have friends over to have a fairy tea party

🐝 laugh and play

🐝 make elaborate fairy pools to cool the fairies down

🐝 make a fairy hotel for all the fairies' visiting guests

🐝 write the fairies a letter

🐝 leave out a small pancake after your family breakfasts

APPEARANCE: Blonde hair, Pointy hat, Blue dress. Blue wing.

CHARACTERISTICS: Friends with a lot of fairys. She is a summer fairy.

FAIRY HOUSE NAME: Beach house

endless. Everywhere you look the world is in full bloom—vegetables, flowers, lawns, fern patches, forests, lily ponds. And all of that growth inspires us to be even more creative!

In summer, you might find a fairy ring, which is a place where fairies meet to dance and sing, usually in the middle of the night. A fairy ring can be a circle of stones, a ring of toadstools, or a circle of thicker, darker colored grass. Do not disturb a fairy ring whatever you do, for they say the fairy queen will immediately take you to Fairy Land and it is much more difficult to get out of Fairy Land than it is to get in. You can make a fairy ring of your own by placing rocks or shells in a circle and perhaps the fairies will have a party there.

What to Collect in Summer

Fairy house materials are every-where this time of year, from bright red poppy petals to delicate Queen Anne's lace flowers. The weather is perfect for gathering sticks, shells, seed pods, and whatever else catches your eye. Trips to the shore are like going to the fairy house version of Home Depot. There you will find the smooth, flat stones perfect for fairy patios. Driftwood can be used for making the structure of a house or for various furniture. Giant clam shells make great bath tubs. Sea glass adds light and sparkle for win-dows and doors. Feathers and even seaweed are great finds for fairy bedding.

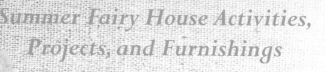

PRESSED FLOWERS

Throughout the height of the season, cut various flowers and leaves to press. Flat flowers such as pansies, black-eyed Susans, daisies, violets, or lavender are the easiest to press. Cut the stems off as close to the flower head as possible. Place the flowers on wax paper and then cover with another sheet of wax paper. Insert the sheets between the pages of a thick book, then pile several other heavy books on top. After two weeks, uncover the flowers and carefully remove them from the wax paper. Save these dried specimens for a cold winter day to create flowery bookmarks, stationary, and gift tags.

MAKE FLOWER PERFUME

One way to capture the beautiful smells of summer is to make your very own flower perfume. Although it is not very difficult, a hot stove is involved, so you will need the help of a grownup to be extra safe. You will need: cheesecloth, flowers, a pot, and water

- Gather the most fragrant flowers in your garden. You will need at least 2 cups of flowers.

- Place cheesecloth over a sturdy pot. Place your flower collection on top of the cheesecloth and cover with water. Let the flowers sit overnight and through the next day.

- Gather the cheesecloth with the flowers inside into a bundle and squeeze any extra water out into the pot of water.

- Put the pot of flower water over medium heat and let the water boil until you only have a few teaspoons left. This will be your perfume! Pour it very carefully into a small glass jar and save for very special occasions.

PLANT A BUTTERFLY GARDEN

Butterflies help pollinate plants when they land to drink the nectar deep inside a flower. Their mouth, also known as a proboscis, is like a long drinking straw sucking up delicious flower juice. While the butterfly drinks, pollen attaches to its body and is carried in flight to other flowers, pollinating them and creating new flowers. Anyone who helps flowers this directly deserves the fairies' everlasting loyalty.

In order to pay tribute to all that these magnificent winged creatures do for the flowers, you can design and plant a garden just for them. Butterflies generally like many of the same flowers as fairies. But while a fairy has an entire language and history, as well as very specific uses for certain flowers, butterflies just tend to like the way flowers smell and their vivid colors. The kind of brilliant and dramatic flowers butterflies flock to require a sunny spot in the garden but one also protected from harsh wind. Several of the plants that butterflies love are perennial, meaning flowers that come back every year. Some of these include: yarrow, coreopsis, purple coneflower (also called echinacea), phlox, honey-suckle, columbine, lilacs, and buddleia (also known as butterfly bush).

To attract that marathon migrator, the monarch, make sure to have some

milkweed in your garden. Milkweed has a tendency to spread wildly due to the large number of seeds in its pods, so it is best to plant it in a wilder part of your yard. In the middle of the summer begin to look under the leaves of milkweed and on the stalk for monarch caterpillars hungrily munching away. This is their main food source, allowing them to fatten up in preparation for their long journey.

FAIRY PLAYGROUND

Fairies love to play, so why not build them a playground? Swings, a see-saw, a slide, a sandbox, and monkey bars are all easy things to build with natural materials.

Swings can be made in a variety of ways. You can find a rectangular piece of bark and loop two pieces of twine around each side. Attach your swing to a frame made out of twigs. You could also use a piece of sea glass or a flat rock for the seat of your swing. A see-saw can be made by balancing a piece of bark on a rock.

Sometimes, a slide already exists in nature. Look for smooth rocks that are at an angle or the base of a tree that has lost its bark. Otherwise, find a smooth piece of bark or a narrow, flat rock and lean it at an angle to create a slide. You can build a ladder for fairies to climb or assume they might fly up to the top of your slide!

Monkey bars can be made just as you would make a ladder, by gluing rungs to two equal-sized twigs. Then make the supporting bars and stand them in the ground.

Fairy Cakes

(Adapted from Betty Bib's
Fairy Handbook)

Many people have fond memories of making fairy cakes with their grandparents. These spongy and delicious mini cakes are perfect for a summer tea party. The best part is decorating them with a sweet glaze and sprinkles, dried flower petals, or tiny candies. This recipe will make about 12-18 cakes depending on how full you fill the cake pan.

INGREDIENTS:
For the cakes:
4 ounces butter, softened
4 ounces sugar
4 ounces self-rising flour
2 medium eggs, beaten
1 teaspoon vanilla
2 tbsp milk

For the butter icing:
> juice of 1 lemon
> 4 ounces powdered sugar

Flavorings:
Vanilla, lemon or orange zest,
almond essence, rose essence

Toppings:
colored crystal sugar, lavender
flowers, sprinkles, candies

DIRECTIONS:

1. Preheat oven to 375°F.
2. Have ready between 12-18 paper muffin cases. These cakes SHOULD be small and dainty and NOT standard "muffin" size.
3. Cream butter with sugar until light, fluffy, and pale in color. Beat the eggs and vanilla and add them bit by bit with spoons of sifted flour. Then stir in the milk.
4. Fill the paper cases half-way with the mixture and bake for about 15 minutes until risen and firm and golden brown.
5. Cool them on a wire rack. To make the icing, put the powdered sugar in a bowl and add the lemon juice. Beat together until the icing is thick enough to stick on the back of a spoon. Decorate with some of the suggested toppings, dust with extra icing sugar, and watch them fly away!

If you have a sand box or live close to a beach, borrow a cupful of sand and use twigs to outline a box shape. Acorn caps are good pails for fairy sand castle building.

DECKS AND PATIOS

Find lots of small, flat rocks to create a fairy patio for your fairy house. You can even make a fire pit for them to sit around to roast tiny marshmallows and sing fairy songs.

SWIMMING POOLS

Add a swimming pool to keep the fairies cool this summer. Clam shells, rocks with a dip in the middle, or even a hole in the ground lined with a hosta leaf all make good swimming pools.

Summer Fairy Houses

SEA SHELL SHANTY

Everybody is at the beach to beat the heat of July, including the fairies. This fairy house is a testament to the great collectibles that can be found at the beach, from sea glass to the

deliciously fragrant *Rosa
Rugosa*. Shells, smooth beach
stones, and sea glass make the
foundation for this sea shanty
that the fairies will use to
refresh themselves after a day
of playing in the ocean.

FAIRY CABIN IN
THE WOODS

The woods in August make a
shady and cool home for fairies on
hot summer days. This house, with
its neatly stacked twig walls and
covered portico, is the epitome of
a Maine woodland camp. The deep
green of the summer forest bounces
off of this tidy little cabin providing
a perfect retreat that will have all
of the forest creatures buzzing
with envy.

WHAT THE EXPERTS HAD TO SAY

Fairies like to swim and climb trees and sit around bonfires. Sometimes, if they want to climb a tree, they look for a kid who is about to climb a tree and they hitch a ride.

In the summer they wear flowers for skirts and dresses and I think they can weave little shirts out of tiny twigs. Fairies like flowers outside their houses, especially roses to keep the danger away (because they have spikes).

Fairies like houses on the beach, high up so it doesn't get washed away. You can look for seashells and starfish and sometimes if you're lucky you can find a crab shell. You can put it in their house, I think they'd like that.

—Tildy

SEASIDE FAIRY CAMP

All along the coast, fairy houses are
dotted in forested pathways. The
fairies gather along the shore to celebrate summer, just like people do!
There are as many ways to build a
seaside fairy camp as you can imagine. The key is similar to the sea shell
shanty, to incorporate shells and bits
of the sea. In summer the fairies like
to spend time together, so making
a large grouping of fairy houses or
a fairy hotel fits the season. Just as
there are an abundance of fairies this
time of year, there is also a ton of
natural materials to choose from to
create this fairy camp.

FALL

"The autumn moon floats serenely over fallen leaves as the woodland fairies eagerly anticipate their autumn festival. Mushrooms grow on the forest floor and leaves turn red, gold, orange, and brown; then flutter gently to the ground ... Harvest moon, gentle moon, stay a little while longer now. Autumn's fairies are gathered to greet you in this bountiful season of gold."
— BEVERLY MANSON

Autumn is a second spring when every leaf is a flower.
— ALBERT CAMUS

Delicious autumn! My very soul is wedded to it, and if I were a bird I would fly about the earth seeking the successive autumns.
— GEORGE ELIOT

Fall

can be as quiet as a gently falling leaf or as loud as the thumping of acorns from a giant oak tree.

There is the cawing of crows and the hustle and scurry of birds and squirrels. Leaves crunch underfoot and apples fall from weighed-down trees. Giant sunflowers lean over and the last blooms of dahlias and mums dance in the autumn light. But it is the changing leaves that win autumn's beauty pageant. The fiery blazes of turning trees mixed with the orange of pumpkins give the world a golden glow. I am always ready for fall after the wild rumpus of summer. But there is a new kind of bustle as geese head south, monarch butterflies head to Mexico, and farmers harvest their crops. Apples are picked, pumpkins are carved, and kids explore corn mazes. It is also time to head back to school, but even so, even with the shorter days and cooler air, there are still fairy houses to build. I think that the fairies love all of this activity, especially when you can create fairy houses that include the golden hues of fall. There is so much to gather this time of year, especially as people put their gardens to bed by pulling up dried-out plants. And all of that gathering and harvesting can be used to build magnificent fall fairy houses.

Fairies in Fall

Quick, look behind that giant sunflower, see that golden flicker? Is that a fairy? Or what about that rustle in the leaf pile? Did you know that the Iroquois tribe believes in a group of fairies called *Ja-gen-oh* who sleep deep in leaf piles to keep warm? According to author Michelle Rohm McCann, "if you scare one out of a nap, it will instantly disguise itself as a dog,

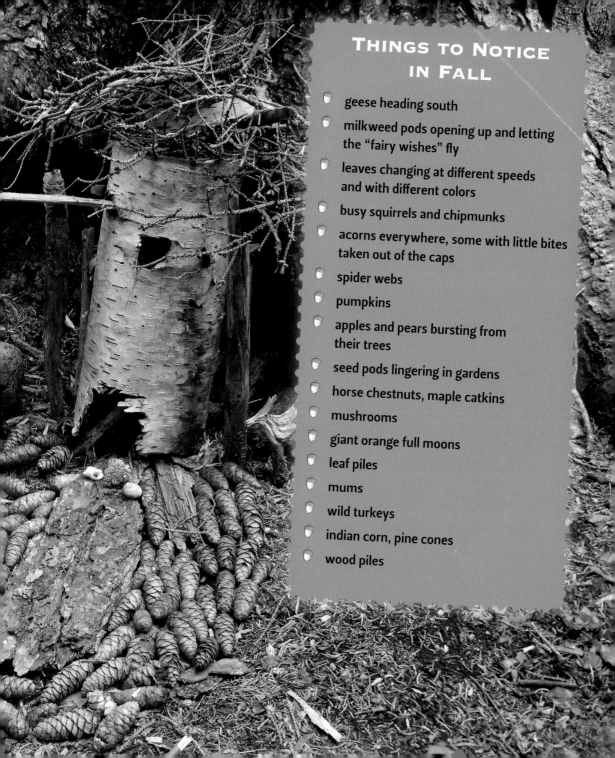

THINGS TO NOTICE IN FALL

- geese heading south
- milkweed pods opening up and letting the "fairy wishes" fly
- leaves changing at different speeds and with different colors
- busy squirrels and chipmunks
- acorns everywhere, some with little bites taken out of the caps
- spider webs
- pumpkins
- apples and pears bursting from their trees
- seed pods lingering in gardens
- horse chestnuts, maple catkins
- mushrooms
- giant orange full moons
- leaf piles
- mums
- wild turkeys
- indian corn, pine cones
- wood piles

butterfly, or blue floating light. If you see one camouflaged as a robin, the Iroquois would say good news is on the way." Bet you never expected that to jump out of a leaf pile!

What do you think it is like for fairies in fall? Imagine only being a couple of inches tall and having giant leaves, acorns, and apples falling every few minutes. Sure you can fly but having a nice fairy house to protect you from all of this falling stuff would be a nice treat. And even though I say this for every season, fall is yet another perfect time to build fairy houses. The choices are unlimited—crabapple cabins, pumpkin houses, or leaf palaces. The abundance of acorn caps means that the fairies have tons of bowls for their fall harvest feasts.

In the fall, troops of acorn fairies, pumpkin fairies, and horse chestnut fairies circle around warm fires. There is even an entire group of fairies known as the Griggs who guard apple trees. According to a young fairy expert I know, the fall fairies have wings like maple leaves. Now, we haven't addressed a big issue in fall and that is Halloween. Fairies are most certainly active on this spooky day and they certainly love all of the children who dress up like them. But mainly the fairies give this holiday over to their creepy cousins, the trolls and goblins. This is not to say that if you create a fairy house in a pumpkin, like the one in this section, that the fairies will not love it, because they certainly will!

SOME EXTRA THINGS TO DO FOR THE FAIRIES IN FALL

- Leave out a thimbleful of soup
- Keep things tidy and rake up leaves
- Support monarch butterfly organizations that help the monarchs on their journey
- Make lots of fairy houses
- Set out acorn caps for the fairies to use in their feasts
- Leave out wool roving and feathers for chilly nights
- Jump in leaf piles, but send a silent message to the fairies that you are coming
- Don't break cobwebs

What to Collect in Fall

As the bright greens of summer fade into the vibrant oranges and reds of the fall, there is much to gather in the woods to add to your fall fairy house. Acorns, pine cones, and birch bark are all abundant at this time of year. There are still plenty of flowers out, especially mums, daisies, and sedum. Gather milkweed husks and the fluffy insides will make soft fairy beds. The whispery insides are traditionally called "fairy wishes." Mums are everywhere in October, as are gourds, pine cones, and scattered leaves. Dried hosta stems and day lily shoots make a great material for weaving together elements of your fairy house.

- acorn caps

- berries

- rainbow colored leaves

- seedpods from spent flowers

- crab apples, gourds, squash, pumpkins

- milkweed pods for baby fairy cradles and fairy bedding

TIP

Often a whirlwind of leaves means there are fairies near and fairy experts say that if you see a leaf falling to the ground, wave to it. If a fairy is nearby, the leaf will wave back.

- dried out cattails

- tiny pine cones and horse chestnuts

- maple catkins

- dried hydrangeas

- dried hosta stems and grasses for weaving together elements of your fairy houses

Fall Fairy House Projects and Furnishings

FAIRY BROOMS

As much as fairies love fall, the constant falling of things keeps them on their toes. With a broom in hand, they are prepared to sweep up the endless droppings of leaves. Find a thin stick and then some pine needles or dried grass. Wrap the pine needles around the bottom of the stick and tie off with a longer piece of grass.

FALL FAIRY BEDS

Unlike the lilac beds of spring, the fall bed is more about comfort and warmth than

Marzipan Toad Stools

(adapted from *Fairy Cooking*)

Fall is the best time to go hunting for mushrooms, especially toadstools. All of the damp, cold weather makes perfect growing conditions for fungi. You might even be lucky enough to find a fairy ring of mushrooms that grow in a perfect circle. This is a sure sign that fairies had a party in that spot! Because you should NEVER eat a mushroom unless you are with a wild mushroom expert, this recipe allows you to make a candy version which might just be a little more tasty.

> WARNING: This recipe uses nuts so do not give a toadstool to anyone who has a nut allergy.

To make 8 toadstools, you will need: 9 ounces marzipan, red food coloring

1. Make two equals halves of the marzipan. Wrap one half in plastic wrap and place the other in a small bowl.
2. Add 3 drops of red food coloring to the bowl and mix it in with a spoon or your fingers (your hands will turn red). Break the red marzipan into 8 equal pieces.
3. Roll each piece into a ball and take your thumb and forefinger and squash them a bit to make a toadstool shape. Press your thumb into the bottom to make a hollow.
4. Unwrap the other half of white marzipan. Take one third of the plain marzipan to use for tiny spots on the toadstools. Press these little balls into the red caps of each toadstool.
5. Break the remaining marzipan into 8 stem pieces. Roll each piece between your fingers and press a red top on it.
6. Store any extra toadstools in an airtight container, but make sure to eat them within 3 weeks.

WHAT THE EXPERTS HAD TO SAY

What do fall fairies do?
— They give warmth to baby wolves by sewing leaves together into blankets using maple stems as needles.

What do they do for fun?
— They use acorn tops for Frisbees and they float chestnut boats down the stream .

Where do they live?
— In the Chinese lantern plants.

— Vera Iserbyt

fragrance. If you fill your bed with milkweed fronds and bits of wool, the fairies will cuddle up and dream away.

A LEAF COVERED TABLE

A table for fairy feasts is an essential for your fall fairy house and is simple to make. You can make a very basic version by sticking four sticks into the ground and setting a red leaf on top. To make your table more secure, you can take four small sticks and glue them into a square, then attach the four legs to create the table. If it is a windy day, a dab of glue will help to keep your leaf on top of your table as well. Then decorate your table with crab apples, fall flowers, and acorn caps filled with berries and little seeds.

TWIG LADDERS

Twig ladders are especially helpful for fairies to use as they climb deep into the heart of a giant pumpkin. Find two straight sticks that are about the thickness of your pinky and about six inches long. Take a skinnier twig and break it into about five pieces of equal length. Using a glue gun or strong white tacky glue, attach each rung of the ladder to the sides.

Fall Fairy Houses

LEAF PALACE

As the bold colors in nature start to fade, the fairies look around for a place that matches the grays and browns of the November landscape. This house is a very traditional fairy house and captures the feel of a November day in the forest. Fairies will love the camouflage of this leafy stronghold.

APPLE TREE CABIN

Fairies are particularly fond of apple trees with their curvy branches and low hanging fruit. They are even used as a doorway to fairyland. The base of an apple tree makes a perfect site for a fall fairy house with tiny crab apples as decorations. Who wouldn't love a house that you could take a bite out of occasionally? In this fall fairy house, that bit of red and yellowish gold matches the fall leaves and makes this house a cozy spot for a fairy to sit and drink a little apple cider.

PUMPKIN HOUSE

By the light of the harvest moon, the fairies will gather inside and around this amazing pumpkin house. Twig ladders lead up to squash ledges where fairies can gaze at the goblins and ghouls passing in the night.

WINTER

"The color of springtime is in the flowers; the color of winter is in the imagination."
—TERRI GUILLEMETS

"I wonder if the snow loves the trees and fields, that it kisses them so gently? And then it covers them up snug, you know, with a white quilt; and perhaps it says 'Go to sleep, darlings, till the summer comes again.'"
—LEWIS CARROLL

"The best snow is the snow that comes softly in the night, like a shy friend afraid to knock, so she thinks she'll just wait in the yard until you see her. This is the snow that brings you peace."
—CYNTHIA RYLANT

Winter

The nip and chill of the air lets us know winter has arrived.

Winter starts with shorter days and the baring of trees. The world quiets itself down as we prepare for more time bundled inside. Soon the first frost paints the world in a sugary glaze, making the grass crunch as we walk over it in the morning. Brilliant fall colors give way to the browns and grays of early winter. The anticipation of snow keeps us on our toes, and when it comes it is like a gift. There is the silence of a snowy morning followed by the scrape of shovels, snow plows, and kids shrieking with joy as they sled down hills. My kids' favorite days in winter are when they hear that they can keep sleeping because there is no school. A snow day is winter's reward. After a big snow, the clear hard blue sky beckons us to come outside. And what better way to spend this kind of day than to go outside and build fairy houses. Sure you can sled, skate, ski, and make snow angels, but as we will discuss soon, winter fairy houses have the added benefit of taking care of the fairies. In this season of giving, could there be a better gift? Not to mention that great feeling of coming inside after playing in the cold all day, slipping off your wet clothes, having a cup of hot chocolate, and warming up by the fire? Don't you think the fairies would love to have the same feeling?

Fairies in Winter

I am very interested in what fairies do in winter. Maybe they sleep the whole winter, hibernating like other winter animals. Or maybe they fly south like geese or monarch butter-flies. But my theory with fairies is that it is always better to be safe than sorry. Just in case they are out there shivering and alone, it is best to build

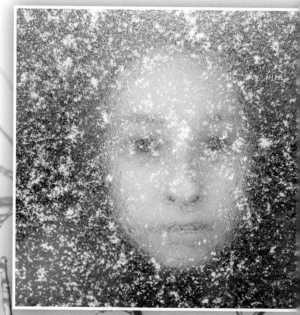

them a fairy house so they know you are taking good care of them. By making them a house at this frigid time of year, you are providing a place where they can rest and take the chill off. And who knows, they might be tempted to stay all winter long, only to emerge when the first flowers appear. As an added benefit, because footprints are so easy to see in the snow, you might even be able to track fairy footsteps and see how often they come to and from your fairy house.

According to the book, *Finding Fairies: Secrets for Attracting Little People from Around the World* by Michelle Roehm McCann and Marianne Monson-Burton, there are

THINGS TO NOTICE IN WINTER:

* animal tracks in snow
* patterns in the ice
* different types of snow: wet, dry, fluffy
* icicles
* different types of buds on trees
* birds eating from feeders
* frosty windows
* leaves and sticks frozen in the ice
* lost mittens
* warm fires
* rosy cheeks
* hot chocolate
* shorter days
* stormy skies
* the shapes of trees when they are bare

many fairies that live and even thrive in cold climates. These fairies dress for the cold in tiny fur snow suits and some even live in miniature igloos! In Greenland, the winter-loving fairies are called *Aua*. According to legends they are on a continuous hunt for a mythic bear that grows bigger when seen by human eyes. In Iceland, these wintry fairies are known as *Huldufolk* and live in invisible villages all over the country.

The most well-known Inuit fairy has a very long name but an incredibly kind spirit. He is called *Kingmingorakulluk*. Roehm McCann says, "this affectionate little fellow loves humans so much that whenever he sees one he bursts into joyful song!" In Iceland, the *Kingmingorakulluk* are known for their amazing sense of direction and channel this ability in order to find lost travelers stuck in the arctic tundra. The young fairy experts I know say that winter fairies have white wings and snowflakes on their clothing. One friend said they have "wings like winter."

What to Collect in Winter

Even though the days are short and cold, fairies really appreciate your effort in winter. Although the snow hides much of the forest, you might be able to find pine cones, sticks, rocks, and feathers; and dried flowers and plants still poke through snowy gardens. Wood piles make perfect scavenging spots for all kinds of bark. As winter comes, it is harder to gather materials outside as the days are short and cold. Look for natural materials in your house to supplement your fairy house collections. Raffia, egg shells, corn silk, and even greens like kale make great additions to a winter fairy house. On top of the snow all sorts of treasures come to the surface—pine cones, birch

EXTRA THINGS TO DO FOR THE FAIRIES IN WINTER

❄ Leave little gifts for the fairies. Fairies love when people leave milk in a little shell or hollow so they can give their fairy babies milk baths.

❄ If you know how to knit, you can make tiny mittens.

❄ Leave out wool roving, wool felt, or scraps of old wool sweaters for the fairies to wrap themselves up in.

❄ Curl up with a good fairy tale to continue to invite the fairies into your life.

❄ Organize your fairy house collections and materials for the upcoming seasons.

❄ Feed the birds—the fairies and birds are very good friends and if you take care of the birds in winter, the fairies will be very happy.

{TIPS}

❆ If you are planning an elaborate fairy house, making as much inside as you can will save you from being exposed to cold weather for too long. It can be a little challenging to do small work with mittens on!

❆ Winter is a great time to organize your fairy house materials and collections. You can also assemble furniture, windows, and doors out of sea glass and branches for your summer fairy adventures.

bark, and evergreen branches are a few of the materials available. One of the beauties of making a fairy house in the winter is that when the snow melts and spring comes, you will find all of your treasures again

Winter Fairy House Projects and Furnishings

MITTENS

The fairies' delicate hands get cold in winter, so having a pair of mittens can be very handy. Perhaps you know how to knit or you have someone close to you who can. You can find patterns for tiny mittens on the Internet. If not, a simpler way to make mittens is to cut them out of wool felt. Remember the smaller the better. You might want to make a practice pair out of paper and then trace that onto the felt. Cut your shape out (you will need two sides for each hand) and then glue the outside edge of the mittens to make two pairs of colorful mittens for the fairies.

Bird-Seed Cookies

Remember what I said earlier, if the birds are happy, then the fairies are happy. Here is a great cookie recipe for the birds and animals in winter! You can make a bunch of these and hang them from a tree. Notice the footprints that come to the tree and you will get an idea of how many different types of animals enjoyed your cookies!

INGREDIENTS: 1 packet pectin, 2 cups cold water, 1 cup flour, 3 cups bird seed.

1. Mix one packet of pectin with two cups of cold water and bring to a boil, stirring frequently.

2. In a large bowl, mix one cup of flour with three cups of bird seed. Add liquid mixture and stir.

3. Fill mini muffin tins with mixture, or form balls by hand. Cut straws into two-inch pieces and then poke into the center of the cookie. This will allow a hole to set in the cookies so you can string a piece of yarn later.

4. Let the cookies set for about six hours before removing them from the muffin tray. Depending on how dry they are when you pull them out, you might need to turn them upside down and allow them to set on the underside as well.

5. Tie a string or piece of yarn through the hole and hang them on a tree for our animal friends and maybe even the fairies to enjoy during the winter.

WHAT THE EXPERTS HAD TO SAY

The winter fairies ride down on the first snowflakes and it is very important that you run outside on the very first snow and leave them gifts.

Winter fairies can live in ice castles, frost castles, or snow castles and also in igloos. They slide down ice hills on frost sleds—you may notice their trails if you go out into the snow first thing in the morning.

They are the ones who make the snowflakes. They fly up into the clouds, grab a ball of water to frost, rub fairy/pixie dust on their hands, roll the ball of water around in their hands, stick one finger in the middle—which makes the branches of the snowflake shoot out and freeze—and then they toss the finished snowflake down to earth.

Winter fairy wings sparkle like the snow.

— Scout

INDOOR FAIRY GARDENS

For those of you who made your fairy gardens in a container, you are in luck! Just bring that lovely display inside for the winter. Not all the plants you used will last due to temperature or light changes, but jade plants or an aloe will love the new inside conditions. You can also add more delicate accessories since the weather won't be wreaking havoc on them. There is a long list of plants that thrive indoors and will do very well in your fairy garden. Baby's tears, English ivy, ferns, and polka dot plants will all look lovely. Watch your fairy garden throughout the winter and tend to it. Give it water, move things around, add new plants if space allows, and come spring, you will know even more about gardening. And who knows, maybe the fairies will even come into your house to visit your garden.

GRASS FAIRY WORLD

If you can't wait for spring, an indoor grass field is a great solution for you and the fairies. You will need a big trough, an old water table, or a shallow rectangular plastic container. Fill with potting soil and then sprinkle generously with grass seed. After a couple of weeks, when the grass is about three inches tall, you can turn your lawn into a fairy world by adding tiny rock pathways and sea glass patios. You can make small bark lean-tos, stick cabins, and whatever fairy houses you can imagine!

POCKET PLOTS

"Pocket Plots" is an activity from the book *What Shall I Grow?* by Ray Gibson. A pocket plot is a tiny garden made in the lid of a peanut-butter jar. First, fill the lid with

a damp paper towel, then gather some sprouting seeds such as mustard or cress. Cover about half of the lid with seeds, leaving the rest for accessories. Cover the lid and keep the paper towel slightly wet. The sprouts will pop up very quickly and then you can add a tiny fairy house and some colored rocks from an aquarium. These make great gifts and you can even eat the sprouts!

ICE ORBS

These brightly colored frozen balls brighten up a white landscape and are perfect for a fairy party on winter solstice. You will need balloons, food coloring, water, and cold temperatures. You simply fill the balloon up with water—trying your hardest not to have a water balloon fight—and add one of the food colors. Then tie the balloon tightly and set it out in the freezing cold or in a large freezer. When the balloons have frozen solid, cut away the balloon (although the material might have already cracked) and you will have a beautiful orb of colored ice to decorate your wintery world.

Winter Fairy Houses

FAIRY IGLOOS

Arctic fairies have long used the igloo as their house of choice during the harsh winters in the tundra. Fairy igloos are almost like a sand castle but with snow and you can use any repeating form to make your structure take shape. In this case, plastic cups were filled with snow and then piled up to form an igloo castle. You could also make a more traditional igloo shape by filling a small rectangular plastic container with snow and then stacking each block. No matter how you make your fairy igloo, the fairies will thank you for helping to build them a winter hideaway to shelter them from the biting winds and cold air.

SNOW CAVES

Who knows if a fairy is shivering out there in the snow storm? Perhaps if you build a simple snow cave, they can duck in and hide out from the ravages of winter. The trick for snow caves is that the snow needs to be deep enough to form a good hollow and not too soft that it will cave in. Once you have a good indentation you can fill it with soft and warm bits like fleece, moss, or feathers. The fairies might also be a bit hungry at this time of year so you can fill an acorn cap with some honey or tiny berries to help fill them up!

LOG CABIN IN THE WOODS

As the bold colors in nature start to fade, the fairies look around for a place that matches the grays and browns of the winter landscape. A traditional fairy cabin in the woods captures the feel of a wintry day in the forest. Fairies will love the camouflage of a leafy stronghold as they nap during a winter storm. A good fairy cabin will keep the winter chill away from tired and frigid fairies. Inside you can add a soft bed made of moss and feathers. Maybe a fairy will be tempted to stay until spring.

Conclusion
Fairy Houses Every Day

There is an old saying that to everything there is a season. After reading this book, that includes fairy house building. As we have traveled through each of the four seasons, I hope you have learned what to gather, what the fairies do in each season, ways to help them, and what types of houses and furniture to build all through the year. You have hopefully traipsed through the woods gathering all kinds of treasures, collecting dry leaves in fall and fresh flowers in summer. Maybe you have made candied violets in the spring and bird-seed cookies in the winter. Or built fairy ladders into your giant pumpkin house.

Whatever activities and projects you have chosen to do, more than anything I hope you've had some wild adventures. Perhaps you've seen fairy

footsteps in the new fallen snow. Or seen tiny scatterings of fairy dust near the entrance of your fairy house. Maybe while building a fairy house, you had the subtle feeling of something watching you. Or all of a sudden a strong smell of flowers wafted over you. These are all signs that you have had a fairy encounter. But maybe your experiences are as simple as noticing the light changing in each season or the way the colors change in the bushes in front of your house. By noticing these very small things, you are becoming a nature detective. Knowing these rhythms of the natural world will keep you right in step with the fairies.

One of my biggest hopes in writing this book is that with each day spent outside doing your fairy work, you will become a caretaker for the earth. The world desperately needs caretakers. The fairies want nothing more than for nature to be valued and protected as much as possible. So remember the fairy code: be kind, respectful, gentle; laugh often; and know that the work you do is helping. Know that the fairies are quietly watching you and they are smiling with wings fluttering, knowing that one by one, children can make the world a better place.

Resources

Books About the Seasons

Usborne Book of Seasons: Things to Do All Year Round by Angela Wilkes

When Autumn Comes by Robert Maass

Fall by Ron Hirshi

Ring of Earth: A Child's Book of Seasons by Jane Yolen

Be Blest: A Celebration of Seasons by Mary Beth Owens

The Artful Year: Celebrating the Seasons and Holidays with Crafts and Recipes by Jean Van J. Hul

Snow by Cynthia Rylant

Around the Year by Elsa Beskow

Fairy Books

Finding Fairies: Secrets for Attracting Little People Around the World by Michelle Roehm McCann

Betty Bibb's Fairy Handbook: A Field Guide to Fairies and Their Habitats by Betty Bibb

A Field Guide to Fairies by Susannah Marriott

Beverly Manson's Fairies: A Celebration of the Seasons by Beverly Manson

Fairy Cooking by Rebecca Gilpin and Catherine Atkinson

How to Catch Fairies by Gilly Sergiev

Laura Ingalls Wilder's Fairy Poems

Fairies and Friends by Rose Fyleman

Fairies and Chimneys by Rose Fyleman